Copyrighted Material

The Digital Real Estate Agent

Building the Brand of You

Blaise Dietz and Michael Mannino II

A Blaise Dietz and Michael Mannino II Publication

First Edition

"Building The Brand Of You" Trademarked

Copyright 2016, Blaise Dietz and Michael Mannino II All rights reserved.

No part of this book may be reproduced in any form or by any electronic or mechanical means, including information storage and retrieval systems, without prior permission of the publisher and author.

Discover other titles and blog posts by Blaise Dietz and Michael Mannino II at
http://www.USAgentCoach.com/

Copyrighted Material

TABLE OF CONTENTS

Foreword

Introduction

Chapter 1: Deconstructing the Digital Marketing Funnel

Chapter 2: Avatar Creation – Laser Target Your Prospect

Chapter 3: Technology That Leverages Both Time and Money

Chapter 4: Understanding Your Digital Assets and the Importance of Branding

Chapter 5: Facebook "FB" Business Page and The Power of The Blog

Chapter 6: Lead Magnets – The Lead Generation Secret of Top Agents

Chapter 7: Generate Highly Targeted Buyer Leads with Facebook Just Listed Ad Campaigns

Chapter 8: Using Facebook to Host a Cost Effective Open House

Chapter 9: The Digital Agent Mindset

Chapter 10: Crush Agent FEAR Like The Cockroach That It Is

Foreword

By: NY Times and USA Today Best Selling Author, Pat Hiban

As a Billion dollar producer and through my podcasts and speaking engagements, I've been blessed to meet thousands of talented, personable, forward thinking real estate marketing professionals. Blaise Dietz and Mike Mannino are two of my favorite, tech savvy digital marketers.

Early on in Blaise's professional journey, at his uncle's real estate brokerage, Blaise made the decision to use technology to help businesses leverage their assets and grow their customer base.

In 1998 Blaise built Michigan's first website, featuring an interactive loan application for a local bank in Northville, Michigan and became known as a digital technology entrepreneur. Throughout his digital marketing career, Blaise has helped build local and national companies with his digital marketing and social media strategies.

I was amazed to think about all that he has accomplished online since 1998...here is one of my favorite stories.

A metro Detroit multi-unit landlord approached Blaise, because he was having a hard time raising capital to purchase a historic building on

Jefferson Avenue, in downtown Detroit, during the real estate crash of 2008.

The Pasadena Building is a 186 Unit, Class C Vintage Apartment building on Jefferson Avenue, and was a pocket listing at the time. The prospective buyer had 30 days to purchase the building, requiring cash payment and zero contingencies. Blaise used social media to raise $2.2 Million dollars in 22 days for the purchase of the Pasadena building.

Blaise's partner Michael Mannino II is a certified digital marketer, and is locally known as the "tax lien" kid. Michael spent the early part of his career working for a master builder, who also happens to be his father Mike Mannino.

Michael started in the advisory side of his father's business, which entails buying distressed real estate assets from banks and other various seller sources. It was fascinating to learn about one of the core strategies that Michael created; to attract sellers who did not want to pay their tax liens off.

Michael purchases tax lien data from the county offices in Oakland County Michigan. He uses the data to digitally target and retarget prospective home sellers, which have fallen behind on their property taxes.

This cost effective digital marketing strategy benefits all parties. This strategy helps sellers walk away with more money at the closing for one main reason.

Instead of waiting for the property to end up at the county tax lien auction, where the seller would have no ability to receive funds from the transaction, Michael shows sellers why it makes sense to sell before it goes to auction.

Digital marketing has leveled the playing field forever.

There has never been a better time to be a real estate agent and investor. With a laser targeted ad campaign, agents can literally been seen everywhere in their local market place. Agents need to build a brand around them; Blaise and Mike understand the importance of that.

The real estate agent *is* the brand...

Digital marketing enables agents to be in front of their prospects and past clients, for a fraction of what print advertising would cost.

This book is about dispelling any myths around digital marketing, and was written as a step by step blueprint for real estate agents. Blaise and Michael help agents realize, that regardless of the size of their advertising budget, they can participate and in many cases dominate the local digital marketplace.

We are not the gatekeepers of data anymore...

Digital and social media marketing strategies have leveled the playing field for agents, by making it affordable to deliver high quality local content to the marketplace, while simultaneously building a brand around you.

Your local marketplace does not want to hear about what sales awards you won last year, or how many homes you sold. Your "on demand" marketplace calls for high quality content that benefits them. As a contributing writer for Inman Select, Blaise had an article published about how to deliver content in the form of a "lead magnet", to grow your most important asset – your list.

I have sold over 1 Billion dollars worth of real estate, am an avid real estate investor and have coached and mentored hundreds of real estate professionals, investors and entrepreneurs through my radio podcast "Pat Hiban interviews Real Estate Rockstars" To succeed in the business of real estate sales, you have to build a brand around you. There is no better way to do that, than by delivering high quality, local market content in the form of a lead magnet.

Blaise's and Michael's passion for digital and social media marketing and for sharing that knowledge is remarkable. The world of digital marketing is constantly evolving.

I hope this book helps to dispel any fear you may have about digital marketing, and encourages you to embrace the future of digital real estate sales with excitement. The best is yet to come...

-Pat Hiban, New York Times and USA Today bestselling author of "Six Steps To Seven Figures -A Real Estate Professional's Guide to Building Wealth and Creating Your Destiny"

Podcast Host "Pat Hiban Interviews Real Estate Rockstars"

Introduction

"If you wait until there is another case study in your industry, you will be too late" ~ Seth Godin

There has never been a better time to be a real estate agent. Digital marketing has leveled the playing field permanently.

Any agent that wants to, can hyper brand themselves in their local marketplace, for a small fraction of what outdated print marketing strategies cost.

It doesn't matter how big or small your brokerage is and it doesn't matter whether you work for a franchise or are a part of the growing ranks of independent agents.

The National Association of Realtors just released recent data that shows how much market share is available for you to capture.

Exhibit 7-1
METHOD USED TO FIND REAL ESTATE AGENT
(Percentage Distribution)

		AGE OF HOME SELLER				
	All Sellers	34 and younger	35 to 49	50 to 59	60 to 68	69 to 89
Referred by (or is) a friend, neighbor or relative	38%	45%	38%	34%	38%	40%
Used agent previously to buy or sell a home	22				21	17
Visited an open house and met agent	5	5	3	5	7	5
Internet website (without a specific reference)						2
Personal contact by agent (telephone, email, etc.)						2
Referred by another real estate or broker						3
Saw contact information on For Sale/Open House sign		78% Of Clients DID NOT use their previous agent				4
Referred through employer or relocation company						*
Direct mail (newsletter, flyer, postcard, etc.)						2
Walked into or called office and agent was on duty	2	2	1	2	2	3
Newspaper, Yellow pages or home book ad	1	*	1	*	1	2
Advertising specialty (calendar, magnet, etc.)	1	*	*	1	1	*
Crowdsourcing through social media/knew the person through social media	*	*	*	*	*	*
Saw the person's social media page without a connection	*	*	*	1	*	1
Other	14	5	9	14	12	20

With a social media marketing budget of $5.00 per day, you can dominate your local marketplace and build a brand around you.

Take a look at the image that we white boarded during a client meeting; it explains why advertising has changed forever.

Your prospect is featured on the right hand side and thanks to the DVR and their mobile device, 99% of the outdated marketing tactics are useless. Consumers have built in "Noise Filters"...

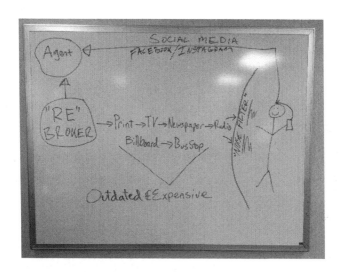

Consumers are now immune to outdated branding and marketing strategies and can filter them out with existing technology. This fact greatly benefits the digital marketing agent.

Your prospects and clients can choose whether or not they want to access to your brand and your content, as you can see in the image.

This book was created to show you how to be fearless and transform your business into a cutting edge real estate digital marketing business.

Your prospects and past clients attention is online and that's where your brand needs to be.

Your clients want a real estate agent to provide localized, highly valuable content and I am going to show you how to deliver that content for dimes instead of dollars.

You can implement all of the strategies laid out in this book within 30 days and have your digital ads running shortly thereafter.

I am an equity partner in a real estate brokerage located in Southeastern Michigan and have been involved in the real estate and real estate finance business since I graduated college in 1995.

Building my first website with Microsoft FrontPage in 1998 and spending hundreds of thousands of dollars on internet and social media marketing campaigns, has earned me a few great successes and several battle scars.

There is no such thing as a "marketing expert", just expert marketing testers.

My partner Mike Mannino and I founded a digital marketing firm in 2015 called USAgentCoach.com. We founded it to help the majority of agents that cannot afford to hire the leading digital marketing firms that charge an enormous amount of money to work with them.

Mike was introduced to me by a local real estate investor as the "tax lien kid". He is a certified digital marketer by the largest digital marketing and training firm in the country and has used his skills to amass a real estate fortune. He attracts 100% of his sellers via digital marketing.

Digital marketing is not rocket science, but it doesn't magically help real estate agents build their most important asset either. A real estate agents most important asset is *their list*.

Mike and I are going to give you the digital marketing blueprints and formulas to help you grow and nurture your list with the types of clients that you want to work with.

Digital marketing allows you to laser target your ad dollars towards the exact type of prospect that you want to work with.

You need to be where your client's attention is, period.

Facebook has over 1.5 Billion daily users; Facebook has the attention of your clients.

Facebook allows you to target your digital ads dollars towards people that live in the zip codes you want to work in, make a certain income level, towards prospects who just had their credit pulled for a purchase mortgage application and so much more.

That's just the tip of the iceberg...

Setting up an automated digital marketing funnel is fun and can be done for less than the cost of a cup of coffee per day.

Where most agents fail, is in the area of follow up. When you are done with this book you will be able to automate your follow up process exactly like the professional digital marketers do.

Exhibit 7-1 above from the National Association of Realtors should be printed in color and posted in your bathroom, bedroom, car and work space.

There has never been a better time to be a digital real estate agent.

Chapter 1: Deconstructing the Digital Marketing Funnel

In this chapter, I'm going to detail a 7-Step Digital Marketing Blueprint that we give to all of our real estate agent clients.

This blueprint will help to lay the foundation for a successful digital marketing strategy.

Don't take notes or get overwhelmed or feel that you don't have enough experience or money to make this happen...you do!

At the end of the book, Mike and I will share the most cost effective resources to make all of these things happen for you.

We will show you exactly how to outsource and hire your own dedicated digital marketing team, who can implement 100% of these strategies and tactics <u>for less than a cup of coffee per day</u>.

These digital marketing strategies will help you quickly separate yourself from the competition during the listing presentation and show your prospects and past clients that you understand how to effectively market their property.

You will also hear us talk about "optics", which is the way you present yourself and your digital marketing plan to your prospects.

The old real estate brokerage models are quickly failing their agents for one main reason. Most brokerages are not delivering any new cost effective social media and local internet marketing strategies that are easy to implement.

If it's not easy and cost effective, agents don't have enough time or money to implement them.

In order to compete with the portal sites like Zillow, Realtor.com and Trulia, which can dedicate large portions of their gigantic budgets to marketing, you need to be smarter about how and where to spend your digital ad dollars.

As I said, you don't need to take any notes here; the rest of the book will give you the granular details and step by step information about how to implement these strategies.

Also, the majority of these tactics can be fully automated and implemented without hiring a web developer or purchasing another useless shiny marketing and technology object.

Again, it's all about the "optics", you need to show your prospects and clients that you're a step ahead of the next agent.

Step 1: Optical Strategy - The Paperless Real Estate Agent

As you already know, we aren't the gatekeepers of data anymore.

You need to make sure that your value proposition, unique selling proposition and most importantly your listing presentation, reflects your understanding of that fact.

Take a look at this chart from the National Association of Realtors.

Today's Home Shoppers are Likely to Conduct Their Research Both Online and Offline

- Real estate consumers who use the internet while researching a home are more likely to use multiple sources
- REALTORS® using offline marketing and sales channels should incorporate digital to complement those efforts

	Used Internet to Search	Did Not Use Internet to Search
Internet	100%	0%
Real estate agent	89	71
Yard sign	53	44
Open house	46	29
Print newspaper advertisement	28	25
Home book or magazine	19	9

100% of home shoppers are able to access all the home data they need from their mobile device. Being a paperless agent is the easiest way to show your prospects and past clients that you get it, that you understand how valuable their time is.

The time to do that is at the listing presentation.

Here's a great statistic that we use as the thesis for our digital marketing plan. It's the single most exciting statistic we use to help agents understand a truth: there has never been a better time to be a digital real estate agent.

Exhibit 7-1 METHOD USED TO FIND REAL ESTATE AGENT (Percentage Distribution)	All Sellers	34 and younger	35 to 49	50 to 59	60 to 68	69 to 89
Referred by (or is) a friend, neighbor or relative	38%	45%	38%	34%	38%	40%
Used agent previously to buy or sell a home	22				21	17
Visited an open house and met agent	5	5	3	5	7	5
Internet website (without a specific reference						2
Personal contact by agent (telephone, email, etc.)						2
Referred by another real estate or broker						3
Saw contact information on For Sale/Open House sign		78% Of Clients DID NOT use their previous agent				4
Referred through employer or relocation company						*
Direct mail (newsletter, flyer, postcard, etc.)						2
Walked into or called office and agent was on duty	2	2	1	2	2	3
Newspaper, Yellow pages or home book ad	1	*	1	*	1	2
Advertising specialty (calendar, magnet, etc.)	1	*	*	1	1	*
Crowdsourcing through social media/knew the person through social media	*	*	*	*	*	*
Saw the person's social media page without a connection	*	*	*	1	*	1
Other	14	5	9	14	12	20

This is the only statistic you should need to get excited about the business of digital real estate sales.

> "78% of all the buyers and sellers in your marketplace will NOT use their last agent …"

First impressions last a long time and they surely affect how prospects will judge you and the next agent coming in behind you.

You need to have your entire listing presentation and marketing plan incorporated into a .PDF or PowerPoint presentation, so you can present to a client on an Ipad or Tablet.

Step 2: Automate the Creation of Single Property Websites with Lead Capture Forms to Build Your List

A second digital marketing tactic, is utilizing web pages to advertise your client's home. Syndicating your listing on portals such as Zillow is an important step; however these websites have the competition of thousands of properties vying for page views all on the same site.

You can automate this process without hiring a web designer and you don't have to break the bank doing it. You can have this done for all of your listings and it can be automated, so that every single existing listing that you have and all future listings that you acquire, have single property websites instantly created.

Having a website dedicated to your client's property has great optics during the listing presentation, and ensures that the property you want to advertise takes center stage.

It also has several hyper local search engine optimization benefits.

A clean, aesthetically pleasing website with lead capture options ensures that you're advertising your client's home, adding leads to your list and doing all of this in a manner which suits the audience you're trying to reach.

There are many additional benefits gained by knowing exactly which prospects were interested in which homes, and segmenting those targeted prospects on to the correct email follow up list.

We cover how to automate your follow up process in detail in Chapter 3.

Step 3: Create Customizable Virtual Tours with Lead Capture Forms

You don't need a video of your client's property either. You can have your still photos turned into a virtual tour automatically.

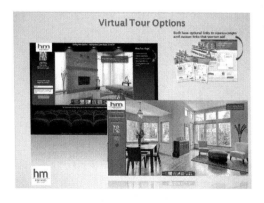

Copyrighted Material

Don't waste your time hiring a web designer or trying to do this yourself. You can fully automate this process and deliver a stunning virtual tour that features a call to action, which is key to your success.

Your sellers will be impressed that your clean, high resolution images or HD video will turn their listing into a commercial.

This "commercial" will be syndicated on all of the popular real estate websites that generate the greatest amount of traffic.

What could be more important than that? It's all about traffic and conversion...

By creating lead capture virtual tours, you now have a legitimate tactic in place to pull prospects off of Zillow and back on to your lead generation pages.

This will also provide you and your team self-generated leads. You can forever stop the lead buying process and generate your own from here on out.

Step 4: Generate Mobile Responsive Lead Generation Landing Pages and Facebook's "Lead Ads" to Deliver Lead Magnets

Lead magnets are ethical bribes used to get prospects to give you their email address or contact information, in exchange for your valuable, localized content.

In Chapter 6 I'll show you how to create lead generating lead magnets in less than 30 minutes, with our 7 step lead magnet check list.

I was honored to become a contributing writer this year for Inman Select, and the first article they published of mine, was about how to properly use lead magnets to generate your own leads.

When you have mobile responsive landing pages working in conjunction with Facebook's ad platform, you have the necessary online assets in place to deliver your lead magnets and build your list.

Again, don't worry about how to do all these things. I'll show you how to fully automate all of these steps for less than the cost of a cup of coffee per day.

Step 5: Use Facebooks Power Editor for Real Estate Agents to Generate Traffic for Dimes Instead of Dollars

By using Facebooks Power Editor to create coming soon, just listed, just sold and open house ad campaigns, you can forever quit wasting your precious ad dollars on outdated and ineffective print advertising.

In Chapters 7 and 8, we will give you the step by step blueprints, of how to put these digital ad strategies into action immediately.

Here's some great data that should get you excited, and inspire you to never spend money on print ads again.

According to Borrell Associates, there was over $6 Billion dollars spent in 2015 on print advertising by real estate sales professionals and organizations.

Over $6,800,000,000 a year!

Let's take look at what the National Association of Realtors says about the effectiveness of print advertising.

THE HOME SEARCH PROCESS

Source - Realtor.org

Exhibit 3-1
FIRST STEP TAKEN DURING THE HOME BUYING PROCESS
(Percentage Distribution)

		AGE OF HOME BUYER				
	All Buyers	33 and younger	34 to 48	49 to 58	59 to 67	68 to 88
Looked online for properties for sale	42%	41%	46%	44%	41%	35%
Contacted a real estate agent	17	13	15	20	21	28
Looked online for information about the home buying process	14	18	14	11	8	6
Drove-by homes/neighborhoods	7	4	5	8	10	10
Contacted a bank or mortgage lender	6	9	7	6	3	2
Talked with a friend or relative about home buying process	5	9	5	3	3	3
Visited open houses	3	2	2	3	4	7
Contacted builder/visited builder models	2	1	1	2	3	2
Looked in newspapers, magazines, or home buying guides	1	1	1	2	2	3
Contacted a home seller directly	1	1	1	1	1	2
Looked up information about different neighborhoods or areas (schools, local lifestyle/nightlife, parks, public transpo	1	1	2	*	1	*
Attended a home buying seminar	1	1	1	*	1	*
Read books or guides about the home buying process	*	1	*	*	*	*
Other	*	*	*	*	*	1

Less than 1% of home buyers looked in newspapers, magazines, or home buying guides.

Again, great news for the digital marketing agent.

Wasting precious ad dollars is actually not the worst part about print advertising when trying to attract new leads and exposure for your clients listing.

The worst part, and I should say the most damaging part about using print advertising in your marketing plan, is that you're telling your prospects that your marketing plan is severely outdated.

Copyrighted Material

Most of your prospects and clients are working for companies that are either thriving or just surviving in the new digital age.

The companies that are thriving are getting rid of *their* outdated print marketing strategies and moving 100% to digital marketing.

When you show up to a listing presentation, with an outdated print marketing strategy, you're going to immediately disqualify yourself as the go to digital marketing agent.

The absolute worst thing you can do at a listing presentation today, is tell your prospective client that you're going to rely on the old 3P's (**P**ut out a sign, **P**ut on the MLS and **P**ray).

Homeowners want one main thing from their agents. They want a marketing expert.

HOME SELLING AND REAL ESTATE PROFESSIONALS

Exhibit 7-6
WHAT SELLERS MOST WANT FROM REAL ESTATE AGENTS, BY LEVEL OF SERVICE PROVIDED BY THE AGENT
(Percentage Distribution)

		AGE OF HOME SELLER				
	All Sellers	34 and younger	35 to 49	50 to 59	60 to 68	69 to 89
Help seller market home to potential buyers	23%	15%	23%	21%	26%	28%
Help sell the home within specific timeframe	20	21	22	25	16	20
Help price home competitively	19	25	20	16	18	15
Help find a buyer for home		12	12	16	15	19
Help seller find ways to fix up home to sell it for more	13		12	15	12	7
Help with negotiation and dealing with buyers	5	5		4	4	5
Help with paperwork/inspections/preparing for settlement	3	4	3	2	3	5
Help seller see homes available to purchase	2	3	2	1	4	1
Help create and post videos to provide tour of my home	*	*	1	*	1	*
Other	*	*	*	*	1	1

*Less than 1 percent

Actually, they want a digital marketing expert. Give them what they want first, and then you'll be well on your way to gaining massive market share over agents and brokerages that do not have digital real estate expertise.

Step 6: Create Digital Mobile Lead Generation and Home Tour Assets For You and Your Client

All of your online assets (web properties) must be "mobile responsive", meaning they have to be easily viewable on all of your prospects' devices.

Having mobile responsive marketing flyers connected to your social media pages is smart, and using QR codes and text for virtual tour codes allows you to satisfy the "I want to see it now" mentality that all home buyers have.

Let's look at some more data...

THE HOME SEARCH PROCESS

Source - Realtor.org

Exhibit 3-8
ACTIONS TAKEN AS A RESULT OF INTERNET HOME SEARCH
(Percent of Respondents Among Buyers Who Used the Internet)

		AGE OF HOME BUYER				
	All Buyers	33 and younger	34 to 48	49 to 58	59 to 67	68 to 88
Drove by or viewed home	75%	77%	78%	77%	69%	65%
Walked through home viewed online	63	65	63	66	60	48
Found the agent used to search for or buy home	30	30	26	28	34	43
Requested more information	24	31	24	18	18	17
Looked for more information on how to get a mortgage and general home buyers tips	13	22	12	7	5	2
Pre-qualified for a mortgage online	13	15	14	14	10	9
Contacted builder/developer	8	7	10	9	10	7
Applied for a mortgage online	8	10	9	8	6	5
Found a mortgage lender online	7	9	6	5	5	5

75% of home buyers drove by, or viewed the homes of their liking, after viewing properties online.

So where do you want to be, when they drive by or view the home? You want to be on their mobile device...

We like to call this young lady in the photo "Sally"…

When Sally drives by the home and decides she likes the way it looks, she wants more information, and she wants it now?

We use a sign rider that looks like this:

And when Sally types in the text to the number, she's going to get a mobile virtual tour sent directly to her cell phone.

She will instantly see the inside of the home, and decide whether or not to request access to the property.

What's great about this? Sally instantly receives what she wants, and also knows that she's working with a digital agent.

She received a link to instant photos, a virtual tour video, and your contact details within seconds!

We manage these digital marketing services for agents all over the country, and because we're data driven guys, we want to know the effectiveness of our strategies.

So we get confirmation of each and every lead that we help generate for our agents.

Here's a screen shot of what our agents email inbox looks like, immediately after a prospect requests an instant mobile virtual tour.

The great thing about this strategy is that it literally costs pennies per day, and the set up time is less than 15 minutes.

There's a great myth out there that digital marketing is complicated and expensive.

Actually the opposite is true.

Digital marketing is a lot of fun and costs about 1/10th the amount of ineffective print advertising. It has the additional benefit of showing your clients that you understand the strategies and tactics to be the go to digital agent.

While transitioning to becoming a digital agent, you may still be buying leads and that's ok, but you need to immediately start automating your follow up process.

It's a simple way to give yourself an edge over the competition.

Step 7: Automate, Automate, Automate Your Follow Up

Let's look at some data that shows that there's never been a better time in history, to be *the* go to digital real estate agent.

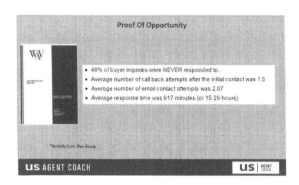

You have to trust me when I say that you can implement all seven steps of this digital marketing strategy for less than a cup of coffee per day, and that should get you super excited.

The image above, which I use during our live presentation, is proof that your market place is ready for total digital agent domination!

Check out the data…

- 48% of buyer inquiries were NEVER responded to
- Average response time is 15.29 hours
- Average number of email contacts was just above 2

- Call back attempts just over 1

Let's look at some follow up facts, from a great marketing data site called HubSpot.

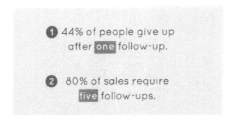

Looks like agents are not the only ones who give up after one follow up. This is great news for those who automate the follow up process.

> 80% of sales require 5 follow-up phone calls after the meeting.

The last slide below is from one of our automation workshops, and will dovetail into the single smartest automation tool ever used by digital marketing agents.

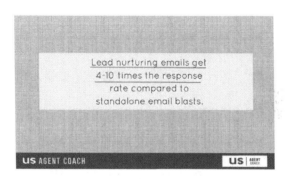

When you automate the follow up process for all areas of your real estate business, you can quickly stack the deck in your favor.

All of the digital marketing data available today supports that statement, and it's so easy to truly automate the follow up process. We set up automatic email communications for our agents using an email technology called Aweber.

The key is to have all of the "call to action" emails handcrafted by you or for you, and we will show you exactly where you can outsource that task for about $7.00 in Chapter 4.

If you do not deliver the correct call to actions, or spew useless information about you or your company in your emails, your leads will instantly "opt out". All of your efforts are then wasted...

I'll show you exactly how to deliver compelling, high quality content, and show you how to have it curated for you.

All you will have to do is localize it, and then cut and paste it into your automated email follow up system. If you don't have a system, don't worry, I'll help you create one.

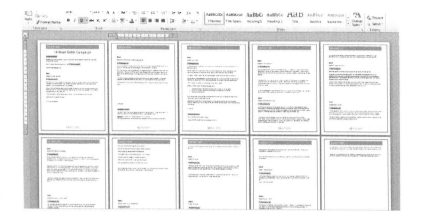

The above image is a 14 week email seller campaign that we hand crafted for our agents.

All they have to do is put their name in the yellow areas, and add some localized information for branding purposes. All that's left after that is to cut and paste them into automated email software like Aweber.

Once that's set up, it's done forever and you've forever automated the follow up process. Remember, lead nurturing emails get 4-10 times the response rate!

That's how you stack the deck in your favor. It can be your edge.

Sit back and get into visualization mode. Picture meeting the next person that says they are thinking of selling their home at your next networking event, or at your child's school function.

Once you implement an email follow up strategy like this, you can simply open up the email application on your mobile device, enter their first name and email and do what our old buddy Ron Popeil says...

"Set It and Forget It"

Take Action Today so that you can profit tomorrow.

Chapter 2: Avatar Creation – Laser Target Your Prospect

> ***"Give me six hours to chop down a tree and I'll spend the first four sharpening the axe."*** Abraham Lincoln

This chapter is all about helping you "sharpen your axe".

So what is an Avatar?

An avatar is a single person who embodies your perfect client or customer. Your avatar is essentially your perfect customer, who is excited to get in touch with you, and your highly sought after content.

Don't worry about content creation in this chapter. I'll show you how to come up with more localized, highly sought after content than necessary.

Let's focus on creating your Avatar first, so that we can create the highly sought after content next.

So why will your prospect avatar be dying to get in touch with you?

Because you're going to provide them with highly valuable information (content), which will help them solve their pain point, and fill the "informational void they are currently experiencing".

I can't stress how important it is to take your time when creating your avatars. If you don't, you'll be putting the cart before the horse, and setting yourself up for failure.

It's imperative to complete an avatar outline for each of your target markets, before you spend one moment working on any other part of your digital marketing plan.

And definitely before you spend any digital ad dollars, it's all about preparation.

If your goal is to generate a massive list of prospects that will eventually become clients, you need to understand exactly who they are.

Creating an avatar for each one of your target markets, will help you laser focus your digital ad dollars, and enjoy a much greater return on your digital ad dollar investments.

Throughout this book you, will hear Mike and me talking about generating your own online leads, growing your most important asset - your list, nurturing your list, and then converting those prospects into closed real estate deals.

Be sure to create an Avatar for each prospect that you want to work with.

Even if you think you already know who your target prospect is…define your avatar.

Defining your avatar will make your digital marketing efforts 10x more effective, and help you deal with the many questions that will come up when implementing strategies throughout the rest of this book.

When going through the rest of the chapters, you will have questions such as:

- What type of content should I create for my blog?
- What should the focus of my content be?
- What problems can I solve for my target prospect?
- What type of lead magnet should I offer my prospects?

Don't worry.

By spending 30 minutes defining each type of prospect avatar that you want to attract to your list, the aforementioned questions will be answered quickly, and help you laser focus your efforts.

So let's create your first Avatar together.

And before I show you how to do that, you want to be thinking of the following, when manifesting prospects to you:

Who is your prospect?

What do they look like?

How much real estate buying or selling experience do they have?

How old or young are they?

What is their average income?

Where do they live, and what areas of town are they most interested in?

Are they married, or part of the fastest growing niche in real estate – single females?

Are they getting divorced?

Do they have mortgage financing experience?

Are they a veteran?

What are they afraid of?

What don't they know about the home buying or selling process that could cause anxiety?

What mistake could cost them both time and money?

What mistakes can you help them avoid?

Remember, this is all about them and not you. It's about solving a pain that they have, or will have during the home buying or selling process.

When you answer the questions above, you will have a much clearer picture of the content that you need to create for them.

You are creating solutions to problems.

They don't care about how many top seller awards you have in your office. It's all about them. Don't be a phony.

Here's the exciting thing to always keep in mind; you're a real estate agent, you have the solutions to your prospects' problems.

You have highly sought after, localized information that your prospect is looking for.

Next, you need to decide what type of clients you want to attract to yourself. To help guide you, I wanted to share some data from a recent special report that was created by the leading media outlet for real estate agents, Inman.

Inman recently released its digital marketing report, "Which Digital Marketing Tactics Provide Bang for Your Buck – And Which Are a Bust."

Remember what I said in the introduction of this book.

"There are no marketing experts, only expert marketing testers"

Use data to help you spend your time and marketing efforts wisely. In other words, don't invent or create new prospect categories to focus on.

Focus on what's working for other first. Put your localized expertise and personal brand into your content, and set yourself up for success.

Top Seven Prospects To Focus On:

1. First Time Home Buyers

2. Homeowners Moving Up to Larger Homes

3. Homeowners Purchasing Second or Vacation Homes

4. Luxury Home Buyers

5. Home Buyers Downsizing

6. Homebuyers Dealing With A Work Transfer

7. Facebook status "Divorced"

And in each of these main segments, there are sub segments that you should focus on:

Zip Codes

Geographical Areas

Age Ranges

Marital Status

Income Ranges

Employees of Certain Types of Companies

Hot & Up and Coming Neighborhoods

Long Standing Highly Desirable Subdivisions

Favorite Vacation Areas in Your State

Lake Front

Mountain View

Golf Course Communities

The list could go on forever, so focus on the type of prospect that **YOU** want to work with.

There's no need to worry about how to laser target your prospects.

We cover that topic in great detail in Chapters 7 and 8. Mike and I will show you how to put your ad in front of buyers who just had their credit pulled for a home purchase mortgage, who live in a certain neighborhood, who make a certain income and so much more.

It's much easier to laser target your audience and create lead magnets for prospects that you are passionate about helping, *after* you have your avatars set up.

It's key to becoming the number one digital marketing agent in your local marketplace.

Let's review an Avatar that we created with one of our real estate agent clients.

A case study of sorts…

This Florida agent is having enormous success targeting baby boomers, which are looking at specific retirement golf course communities in Florida.

Step 1: Start by defining which one of the "Top Seven Prospects to Laser Focus On"

Prospect Avatar – Homeowners Purchasing Second or Vacation Homes

Age Range: 62 -72

Gender: Male and Female

Marital Status: Married

Number of Children: 2

Primary Residence: Michigan

City They Currently Reside In: Birmingham, Michigan

Goals: To purchase a home in "The Founders Club" in Sarasota Florida this year.

They want the peace and quiet in an area that's removed from the typical hustle and bustle, but also conveniently located to a variety of dining options, entertainment and a culture that they believe Sarasota offers them.

Values:

Would like year round access to a retirement community with like-minded individuals, that's also welcoming to the children and pets.

Desires to interact with the neighborhood and community.

Challenges:

Has never owned in Florida, and not sure exactly which community is best suited for the family.

Pain Points:

Considering a long distance new construction project in a golf community is causing some anxiety.

Anxious about dealing with a new construction project.

Sources of Information:

Fortune Magazine

Books

"Live Life to the Fullest and With a Lot Of Fun"

"The Birds of Pandemonium"

Websites: Entrepreneur Magazine

That's how you create an avatar, which helps you laser focus on the target market you're interested in. Sharpening your axe…

It's time to create your Prospect Avatar. You can do it by going through the exact same process we just reviewed together.

Can you see the benefits of creating an Avatar for all of the prospects that you want to work with?

Creating an avatar right now will prepare you for Chapter 6.

In Chapter 6, I will show you how to quickly create the "ethical bribe" that will get your prospects to give you their contact information, in exchange for your highly valuable content or "lead magnet".

In the coming chapters you're also going to learn how to laser focus your ads to attract the exact type of prospect that you're looking to work with.

How cool is it that Facebook's three ad platforms allow you to laser target your prospect by age, income, zip code, desired neighborhood, those looking to purchase and so much more.

No more wasted ad dollars!

We are professional marketing testers, and you should be also!

Digital marketing technologies and marketing tactics are constantly evolving, and that's a great thing for you!

It's your edge over the competition.

Chapter 3: Technology That Leverages Both Time and Money

You'll remember in the beginning of the book where I stated that Mike and I are data driven guys. It's so easy to be talked into buying the next shiny marketing or technology object that promises to deliver "7 new listings per day".

Do yourself a favor and commit to becoming a digital marketing agent, and you will never be fooled again.

I am going to cover three core technologies that every single agent must use if they want to "stack the deck" in their favor, and take advantage of the data that we shared with you in Chapter 1.

You don't have to use these exact technology vendors, but you need to use something that helps you leverage time effectively, and keeps your brand looking professional.

Here are the three technologies that we are going to cover in this chapter.

- Aweber – Using email autoresponders to become "follow up experts"

- Dropbox – Leverage your time by accessing every single file on every device

- Canva – Perception is reality, and if you want to be perceived as a pro you need to look like a pro

Let's start out by reviewing some data provided by HubSpot to hammer home how imperative it is, to become a master of the follow up.

Then, I am going to show you how to automate the follow up email process once and for all.

> Lead nurturing emails get 4-10 times the response rate compared to standalone email blasts.

That's the great thing about data; you don't have to guess as to whether or not you should invest your time into setting up an automated follow up process.

From HubSpot…

> Businesses that use marketing automation to nurture prospects experience a 451% increase in qualified leads.

It's also important to review some data that we received from the Wav Group.

Hardcore follow up data:

- 48% of buyer inquiries were NEVER responded to

- Average number of call back attempts after the initial contact was 1.5

- Average number of email contact attempts was 2.07

- Average response time was 917 minutes (or 15.29)

Those statistics should excite you more than any other piece of data in this book.

Why? It's like having a crystal ball telling you exactly where to focus your efforts

Follow Up, Follow Up, and Follow Up!

Mike and I will show you a dozen different ways to generate new leads every single day, but they're totally useless if you're not fully committed to following up.

The great news is, follow up is one of the easiest things to do if you're willing to invest a small amount of time up front.

One of the most user friendly follow up tools that we use for our clients is Aweber. It's for the beginner, and it's super user friendly.

Aweber is one of our favorite tools at US Agent Coach, and I bet it will become one of yours also.

"Our core focus is to help you learn how to generate your own online leads and nurture them until they become clients."

Aweber was created to automate all of your email marketing needs.

All you have to do is write the emails (or have them written for you) and load them into the correct Aweber prospect avatar list. With Aweber, you can create a new list for each type of prospect that you are marketing to.

Once that's done, you're ready to add your prospects and clients onto your lists.

You will also enjoy the peace of mind that comes with knowing that your prospects are being followed up with automatically.

After you complete Chapter 6 on Lead Magnets, you will understand our core strategy for adding daily subscribers or leads to your email list.

Our core strategy involves giving away a lead magnet or something of great value to your targeted prospect in exchange for their email address.

That's how you build a massive list of leads!

How are you going to use the follow up data we've been sharing with you as your edge over every other agent?

Answer: your follow up process will dwarf what the competition is currently doing.

This is not following up enough, if at all.

Aweber

Here's how Aweber works:

You create specific list titles in Aweber, and the list titles should be congruent with your target prospect Avatar name.

If you're targeting first time homebuyers, which still make up a third of the market, then your list name will be "First Time Homebuyers" so on and so forth.

There are only two steps to this entire list creation process and we timed it. It takes less than 60 seconds to create each one.

After you click the next step button, you will decide if you want your prospect to confirm their email subscription, before Aweber automatically emails them your lead magnet.

The follow up email series that will begin after the first email is sent, is called the "Legacy Follow Up System".

Legacy Follow Up System is just a fancy name for a series of emails.

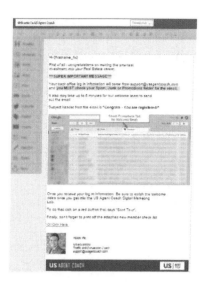

In the above image, you can see our original welcome email that will be sent once someone becomes a "Done for You" client of USAgentCoach.com

It has the subject header and the body of the email. In the body of the email, you can insert text, images and links to anywhere you want to guide your prospect or client to.

There's also seven other emails that we have written, which are automatically sent on specific time intervals. So every time we have a new client join, we don't have to worry about sending them the correct email.

Do it once, and it's done forever.

Mike and I love Aweber for our clients in comparison to every other email autoresponder service out there.

It's for beginners, and their free live support is second to none.

Every great agent needs a team behind them.

If your broker owner is not able to offer you access to a digital marketing team, you can contact our team for help.

Many of our agents do not like to write emails or blog posts, and in Chapter 4, we cover the best ways to outsource these tasks like the pros do.

You can outsource a lot of these writing tasks to companies like Iwriter, where you can get your articles written for about $10.00

You have to deliver great content in your follow up email series to your prospects. If you don't, the lead that you worked so hard to get onto your list, will request to be taken off of your list.

The difference between delivering hand crafted emails that speak directly towards the prospects known desired result, and some canned reply, is a stark difference.

People's bullshit detectors are on high, due to the massive amount of shiny objects shoved in front of them every day.

Promising to deliver a dozen new listings per month, or automatically writing emails for you in your sleep offers, have numbed the agents' skull. Just say no!

Delivering quality content is an easy way to dominate your local marketplace. You will be one step closer to becoming the go to local real estate authority.

You saw the statistics earlier. It takes several contacts to properly nurture a lead, incubate it, and then birth it into an actual client.

We write all of our follow emails for our clients. They know it has to be done correctly, to maximize the chances of converting their prospects into clients.

Here's a look at our 14 Week Seller Campaign Email Series…

All our agents have to do is plug in their personal information into the highlighted areas and let our team load them into the Aweber platform.

The point is: automate, automate and automate some more!

Once you do that, you're well on your way to using the data that we've been sharing with you, to stack the deck in your favor.

The next section in this chapter will cover a very simple technology tool, which will help you leverage your time and stay organized.

Dropbox is the name of the tool.

Benefits for Real Estate Agents

- All of your documents are always backed up and saved – never lose a file
- Ability to access documents, files, folders, images, videos,

- Ability to share any size file, on any device, at any time, with anyone
- Ability to become a true paperless agent
- Ability to manage all of your team documents, and set permission types for editing and sharing

Imagine always being able to access any document, image, video, contract and listing presentation on any device that you own: Mobile phone, Ipad, tablet, personal computer or Mac.

All of your files on all of your devices.

When I need to get a presentation that I've created at the office, to present or send to a client, all I have to do is complete three simple steps.

Step one: Click on my mobile Dropbox application

Step two: Select the folder that I want to access

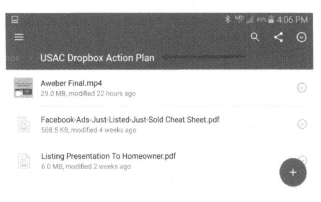

Step three: Select the file I want to access or send out

Copyrighted Material

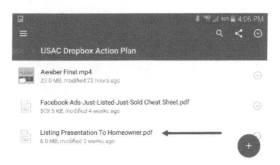

Once I click on the file, in this case the PDF, I can view it in its original format, and move from page to page with the swipe of a finger.

No more asking assistants to email you anything. All your files are always with you, and always backed up.

If you want to share any file, just click on mail or message or copy a link and then send it to anyone you know.

"If you want to be viewed as a digital marketing professional, you have to play the part, and look like a professional."

Canva

The first online impression your prospect sees, tells them about your level of professionalism.

If you don't have a great online brand or image, you most likely won't make into the batter's box. You won't even get a swing of the bat, or a chance to win the listing.

Perception is reality. You can fix that with ease if you are willing to use one of our favorite free tools called Canva.

Canva is your personal graphic and image designer, and yes you can use it totally free.

There's so much more to Canva, but I'm just going to share the basics with you.

When you need a professional cover for your listing presentation, a background image for LinkedIn or Facebook, or just a simple cover for your highly sought after "lead magnet"…just open up Canva.

It's so expensive to hire or outsource your image work to a designer, and it's never looks exactly as you envisioned it should.

Unless you have an in house designer at your brokerage, Canva is the simple solution to your digital image problem.

You can take any image of yours or theirs, and quickly cut and paste your logo onto it, add text, change fonts and so much more.

Showing is better than telling. Let's take a quick look at how we used Canva to design a Facebook image, which was being prepared for a Facebook ad.

The editing panel is on the left and the image we uploaded from our computer is on the right.

We wanted to get Mike's mug, which only a mother could love, put onto the image. All we had to do was upload the image of Mike, and then drag it into place.

Next we needed to brand the image with the USAgentCoach.com logo.

Then, we wanted to add a call to action, at the bottom of the image.

So we added the green bar. All that was left to do was to type over the text that says "Add Subheading". Canva even tells you what and where to place your text.

Here's the final ad that's been generating leads for us from day one.

Use Canva to quickly brand yourself, and tell the marketplace that you are the go to digital marketing agent.

In your ads, on your listing presentations, for the images on cover of your lead magnets, Canva should be in your digital marketing toolbox.

Chapter 4: Understanding Your Digital Assets and the Importance of Branding

Building your brand, and promoting that brand on your digital real estate assets the correct way is critical. Preparing to make the most out of a digital lead generation strategy is what we're going to cover in this chapter.

Keeping it very simple is my primary goal, so that you can execute on these items confidently, and have them in place quickly.

If you already have a great online brand presence, and a high converting sales funnel, congratulations!

You should still be able to pick up on some good ideas, and improve upon your existing digital assets.

We are going to focus on two core areas:

- Your Digital Assets

- The Importance of Branding or "Optics"

Your Digital Assets

Remember, there's no such thing as expert marketers, just expert marketing testers.

As an aspiring digital marketing testing expert, you need to get your online presence (sales funnel) in place, otherwise you are putting the proverbial cart before the horse, and setting yourself up for frustration and failure.

Before you can create an ad, send traffic to the ad, and get clicks to your lead capture page, you have to have the basics in place to capture those leads.

Your online digital marketing funnel can be created and deployed in less than 30 days, and for less than $1000.00. It should not be a complicated process.

After your funnel is in place, you will be ready to drive traffic (avatar prospects) into your sales funnel, and test your conversion strategies.

Setting up your online presence and brand properly is fun, but the real fun begins when you start sending low cost, highly targeted traffic into your funnel.

From there it's just test, test, and test some more, until you find the proverbial honey hole.

We never spend more than $3.00 - $5.00 per day testing our sales funnel, and neither should you.

Simplified Sales Funnel

After you identify your best converting funnel, is when you turn up the ad spend.

"If you put a quarter into a machine and it spits out a dollar, how many quarters will you put into that machine?"

There are four primary online lead capture pages that we send traffic to, once the target prospect clicks on an ad.

Although the branding begins with your digital ad, it's equally important that your other online assets are congruent with your ads.

1. Facebook business page posts and Facebook custom tabs

2. Landing pages – we use Clickfunnels.com

3. Blog posts

4. Single property websites

In Chapter 2, I showed you how to create an avatar for each type of prospect that you want to target.

Once your digital assets are set up and in place, you will target your avatar with your ad.

Once the ad is clicked, the prospect is sent to your delivery page, and from there you will track lead conversions.

A conversion happens when your prospect takes the desired call to action.

Your primary call to action, on the page that your traffic lands on, will be asking for the prospect's contact information. They will give you their information because you're going to present them with the ethical bribe, or "lead magnet".

Blaise Dietz is a real state digital marketing and technology coach. He blogs about real estate digital marketing strategies and technology tools on his blog at USAgentCoach.com

Recent Articles by Blaise Dietz

5 steps to creating magnets for generating leads online

The lead magnet is the most important part of the lead generation or list building process. Without a great lead magnet, it's very challenging to start or grow the most important part of your business: your contact list .....

By Blaise Dietz | Tuesday, January 5, 2016

I had an article published about lead magnets at a leading media outlet for agents called Inman Select.

I'll go into some depth about the power of lead magnets, and the exact execution strategy we use to deploy them in Chapter 6.

<u>*"There is no secret to generating online leads"*</u>

The companies that sell leads to agents use the exact same strategies and tactics that we do, and you can also.

There are proven digital marketing sales funnel processes that work. That's why it's critical to avoid wasting resources trying reinvent the wheel.

When you create a solid foundation, you set yourself up for success and stack the deck in your favor. By removing 90% of the digital marketing challenges most agents face during the preparation phase, you will make the most of your time.

Branding and "Optics"

While reading the Financial Times, I found the best way to define the "Optics" of your personal brand.

It was written by Lucy Kellaway.

Her translation into plain English:

"How You Come Across"

She went on to say...

"Managing the optics of your personal brand image...whether in public or private, managing the optics of your brand image means being constantly aware and thinking that your brand is always on stage"

That sums it up.

As a real estate agent, you're always on stage and being judged, especially at the listing presentation.

Just like it doesn't make sense to go to a listing presentation in your gym clothes, the same goes for the optics of your online presence.

You can't go to a listing presentation and tell your prospect that you're a real estate agent, with digital marketing expertise, and have a website from 2005.

Your online presence has to be easily viewable on every device, and it has to be professional.

When you have a professional personal and business image, your confidence goes up exponentially. You walk differently, you talk differently and it's no secret, people do business with confident people.

What I'm about to say next is going to sound fancy, but it's actually stupid simple to pull off, and it will instantly show your clients that you are a digital agent.

It's the easiest way to say "I am cutting edge".

"Become a Paperless Agent"

You should never walk into a listing agreement with any paper except a notepad and an Ipad or laptop.

The entire listing presentation should be digital.

At the presentation, show your clients data which supports your digital marketing plan. You will prove to them, beyond a shadow of a doubt, that marketing their property digitally is the smartest way to sell their home fast, and for top dollar.

The optics of a digital listing presentation is awesome, and it's a simple cost effective way to stack the deck in your favor. It sets the bar extremely high for the next agent coming in behind you.

In the next chapters, Mike and I are going to give you a step by step action plan, so that you can start putting everything that you have learned so far into practice.

We give away our digital listing presentations that our agents use on our weekly online workshops, and show you how to put them together in 30 minutes or less.

You can register for our next free workshop by going to www.usagentcoach.com

Chapter 5: Facebook "FB" Business Page and The Power of The Blog

We just finished talking about the importance of having a basic digital marketing funnel, and the importance of your "Optics".

It's time to get super excited and set up one of your most important digital assets, your Facebook business page. You cannot place any ads on Facebook without one.

But first, I want to share something from one of the top companies in our industry...

The Keller Williams's website said it best when they shared what they believed was an industry secret and I agree with them.

From the KW website:

"Most Important Secret Of the Real Estate Industry"

"Whenever an agent switches from one brokerage to the next, their clients follow. YOU are the reason people do business with you and you should build your career on this fact! At Keller Williams Realty, we recognize that the agents are the reason we do business."

They nailed it!

In case it's not crystal clear, your real estate brand needs to be built around you!

People do business with the agent because of whom they are and that's why I teach all of our agents, how to build a brand around them.

One of the easiest and most cost effective ways to get your brand set up properly is with a Facebook business page.

Facebook won't let you put an ad in front of your target market without having a business page. Let's get your business page set up and branded properly, so that you don't put the cart before the horse.

I'm going to show you how to quickly and professionally set up your page and this will accomplish multiple things for you.

We tell all of our agent clients that the smartest and fastest way to start or update your digital online presence or optics, is to make sure you FB business page and your blog is set up professionally.

If you really want to grow the size of your most important asset, your list, you should have both a business page and a blog. Both the FB business page and the blog should be set up and ready to go before spending any digital ad dollars.

These two assets will be the foundation of your content delivery system. It will be there to deliver all of your highly localized content and allow you to brand yourself, as the go to digital marketing agent.

Once they are both set up properly, you can automate about 80% of the content that you need to place on them.

Let's start with Facebook

Facebook Business Page Essentials

I am going to take you through some of the set up basics and then show some visual examples of how it should look when you're done. After that, I'll point out how this benefits you!

The name of your Facebook business page is searchable through Facebook and Google. You want to make sure that your page name reflects who you are and what you are doing in the marketplace.

You will start this process by signing into your personal Facebook account.

Next, you want to hit the small drop down arrow in the top right of your home page and then select "Create Page".

WARNING: You should NOT include the name of your current company in the title of your page unless you are the broker owner. Remember, the brand is you and if you leave your broker, you don't want to have the company name branded into your page URL.

You can only change it once. More on that in a minute...

In a moment, I'll show you where to put your company logo if you want to use it. We need to finish naming your page, as it's a very important step in the branding process.

If your name was Julie Smith you would use something like "www.Facebook.com/JulieSmithRealEstateProfessional".

You can only change your Facebook name once, so be smart and be sure to keep the brand all about you!

Ok, so after you name your page with your real estate branded name, you need to promote your page in your personal Facebook page and website.

Quick tip: Never promote you; promote your highly valuable content!

Agents can get so uptight and be so phony when they think about building a brand around them. Be careful, if you don't know how to build a brand around you by giving away highly valuable localized content, then do not start promoting your page until you read the next chapter.

People can smell a phony from a mile away.

The way you promote a brand around you, is to deliver high quality, localized content in the form of a free lead magnet and I cover Lead Magnets in depth in Chapter 6.

I'll show you how to have fun with social media, while giving away really cool content.

For the agent's pages that we manage, we help them keep it fun in a quick and simple way.

We do fun things for their audiences like having really cool sweepstakes and giving away gift cards to Home Depot and Bed Bath and Beyond. In addition to fun things like that, we use our agents Facebook business pages to give away highly sought after Lead Magnets (content).

Be fun, be vulnerable, be real and give away content that makes your audiences beat a path on to your list!

So after you have named your page you want to select "Brand or Product" and "Product/Service" in the dropdown menu.

And the reason for selecting this and NOT the local business or place, is that 99% of the time when you meet with a client, you're meeting at their home, and not at your office.

You do not want to promote your "address" as much as you want to promote your service!

Next are the page description boxes.

The first information box is asking for a short description. In the short description you want to tell people who you are and what you do, and what local area you specialize in.

The second box is asking for your personal website. In this box you also want to link the URL to your personal website blog. If you don't have one, then have someone build a small professional blog site for you, ask our team to do it for you, or use your office site until your blog site is built.

The third box is asking for your Facebook URL. This is where you will place your personally branded URL that we discussed a moment ago.

Once that is done, click "Save Info" when you are finished.

For your profile picture, you can either upload one from your computer or from your website. If you don't have one, get that done!

You want to upload a professional well-lit photo of yourself, and not one that's taken at the bar …. or the morning after the bar either. lol

Then you will hit "Save Photo".

Next, you want to add this page to your favorites.

Now you want to enter in the location you want to service, and you should have this set for at least a 15 mile radius or greater.

Now that you have the foundation set up, let's work on making this look professional.

You need to add a cover photo to your page, which will really make this page look professional, remember "optics". You can always look at the one we used in the beginning of this chapter to give your web team some inspiration. If you don't have a digital marketing team, we will be your digital marketing team.

To add a cover photo, upload one from your computer. The image size should be around 850x315 pixels.

Next, let's set up your call to action button. The first step is to select the "Create Call to Action" button.

We can now choose what the button says, "Book Now", "Contact Us", "Send Message", "Show Now", or "Sign up" and whatever else Facebook adds to these options over time.

You can leave it as "Contact us" and when a prospect clicks on the button, you can choose what online asset or website you want it to take your prospect to.

At US Agent Coach we help our agents create their own online assets. We suggest that they link to a landing page of theirs, to deliver a seasonal lead magnet, or to a specific blog post which essentially tells the reader, "I'm the local area expert".

Then hit "create"

I highly recommend going through each section of your FB business page and adding information about you. Try using local keywords in your text, by doing this it will help with the local SEO (search engine optimization).

The more local key words you use, the more likely your Facebook profile will show up on Google's first page, when someone is looking for a local agent expert like you!

Now that you know how to set up your FB business page and branded profile, I want to show you some quick ad examples and some results of those ads. All coaching and no case studies make for a boring book!

We recently ran a very simple "what's my home worth" ad for HomeMark Realty Group and set the daily ad spend to $3.00 per day for our test. The ad looked like this.

Here are the results that came from the ad...

That ad generated 108 leads, at a cost of .027 a piece, which ended up getting us in front of four prospective home sellers, that wanted to meet with an agent to discuss listing their home.

When you have professional posts or ads set up properly, you can drive traffic to them for $3.00 - $5.00 per day. Again, you are accomplishing multiple goals at the same time. You're making the most of social media marketing and lead generation, while at the same time branding yourself.

And remember, there's no such thing as a professional marketer, just professional marketing testers.

Testing your own lead generation strategies takes no more than 30 minutes and $3.00 per day. It's a lot more fun than cold calling or working the same leads that every other agent in town is working.

All of your ad strategies should always build a brand around you because "optics" matter.

Remember, when you have the right optics, you also tell your prospect that you're already a professional digital marketer.

It gives you the opportunity to talk about your real estate digital marketing plan or "secrets".

Prospects that read your zero bull!#*%, highly valuable, localized content, will be excited to invite you over to show them more details your digital marketing plan.

Picture walking into your next listing appointment and getting a compliment from your prospect about how helpful your information was. They go on to say how cool it was to find you on Facebook and now get to see you in person.

You're the local digital marketing expert and that's exciting!

In the next chapter, I'll go into detail about how to create informational "lead magnets" in the form of reports, check lists and "blueprints".

These ethical bribes work like magnets to get prospects on to your list, and eventually get them to request an in person meeting, if you create them properly.

Blogs do you really need one?

The short answer is yes. Why? Let me share a discussion I had with a top agent in town last week, before I tell you why you need a blog.

I spoke with "John", who's an agent with the top agency in Birmingham, Michigan. This agency is number one in the State for both deal volume and number of units closed.

"John" closed over 30 Million dollar's worth of business last year and is one of the most sought after agents in town.

We spoke about the current state of the real estate business, and he agreed that digital real estate sales are the future of the real estate business. Here's why…

There are two main reasons that he cited for this. He related it to one of his greatest concerns for agents that do not have a business like his, a "by referral only" book of business.

"Blaise, as you know we are not the gatekeepers of data anymore."

And he went on to say "The days of sitting in another agent's open house, or taking incoming calls or walk-ins during "floor time" are over.

There's no easy way to build a book of business offline anymore, and that's a fact."

It's actually great news for digital real estate agents that commit to doing business in the digital world. This is *the best time* for new agents to build a book of business online. You can do it yourself or have it all done for you without breaking the bank.

When someone is looking to move, and wants to find out what their home is worth, they whip out their mobile device and search. It doesn't matter what you think about the quality of online property evaluation tools, your prospects are using them.

When a first time home buyer wants to check out home prices in the city they want to live in, they pull out their mobile device and search.

Look at every car that you drive by today with a passenger in it, where's their head...down in their mobile device. And that's why your brand needs to be on their mobile device, because that's where your prospect's attention is.

Remember, you can laser target your exact avatar or prospect on Facebook. You don't have to waste ad dollars guessing where their attention is at.

That's why a blog is necessary. You can laser target your prospect with an ad, and when clicked on, it will send them to your blog post. For pennies a day, you can effectively brand yourself as the go to digital marketing agent.

When you drive your targeted prospects to your quality content, you have a high probability of adding them onto your email list. They will want to stay in touch with you. Why...because you're delivering highly sought after, localized content.

The blog is the agent's perfect delivery vehicle for high quality, hyper localized content. Remember, you don't need to sell anything on your blog; you need to use blog posts to demonstrate your local expertise.

We drive traffic to our blog posts via Facebook ads, for less than $5.00 per day, and they generate leads for our agent clients.

There are two main push backs we get from agents that are concerned about starting a blog:

First, they don't know how to create a professional looking, mobile responsive blog, and second, they state that they're not good writers or don't know what type of content to share.

To solve the first challenge, you need to have a blog developed for you that looks professional, brands you, is connected to you or your market MLS via an IDX feed and doesn't break the bank.

Be careful when choosing a digital marketing company to create your blog or any other digital assets for that matter.

Most agents can't afford to work with companies such as Curaytor or Boomtown that at the time of this writing, charge over $1000.00 up front for your site, and even more for their monthly support.

You can get that done for less than $1000.00 up front, and monthly digital marketing support for less than $100.00 per month; if you are willing to participate in the content and ad creation process.

Real estate is a local business, and you are trying to brand yourself as the local expert, right? If that's your goal, then you have to contribute to the content. You want to be perceived as genuine and truly offer highly sought after information. I am not saying that you cannot outsource content creation, but you have to be the final editor of that content.

Be careful of the big fancy firms when agreeing to any sort of contract. There's no need to be locked into a contract where *you can never leave*. It does not have to be "Hotel California" – may God rest Glenn Fry's soul.

Did you know that the biggest vendors in the country will not let you leave them; will not let you take your website with you?

Be sure to ask for their "break up process", and make sure it's clearly written that you own your site.

When it comes to generating ideas for your content, there's good information about how to accomplish that on our blog.

Creating Content

Now if you're afraid of writing your own blog posts, don't be, I have an awesome solution for that. Have you ever heard of Iwriter.com?

At Iwriter, you can have an article written for you for less than $10.00.

We also wrote a blog post about how to work with Iwriter, but I can summarize it for you here. Go to Iwriter and set up a free account, tell them what you want your article written about, and then order it up.

The article will be delivered back to you within a couple of days, and in some cases hours. Here's the best part, you only pay for the articles that you approve.

Once you approve an article, you can download the article and then there's only two steps left from there.

You have to localize your article with your knowledge of the marketplace. Once that's done, all you have to do is cut and paste it into your blog and hit publish or submit.

If you need help getting this done for you, we can help.

There's one more resource that I want to share with you called UpWork. At UpWork you can find great writers, bloggers and other content creation helpers. You can also review a copy of their work product before you hire them. In the next chapter we're going to talk about one of my favorite content topics, and that's "Lead Magnets".

They truly are the most effective way to generate your own leads, establish your local expertise, and help you make the most of a $5.00 per day Facebook ad campaign.

Chapter 6: Lead Magnets – The Lead Generation Secret of Top Agents

I'm going to show you exactly how real estate agents use Lead Magnets to generate online leads and how you can also.

If you want to grow your prospect avatar list, you've got to offer an ethical bribe that's highly valuable in exchange for their contact information.

Key Takeaways

- The goal of the lead magnet is to convert your social media and digital marketing ad spend traffic into a lead. Think list building.

- You must offer something deemed highly valuable on your Facebook business page, landing page or blog, to ethically bribe your visitor for their contact information.

- Lead magnets should be easily consumable and the first entry point into your digital marketing funnel.

The lead magnet is *the most important part of the lead generation or list building process.*

Without a great lead magnet, it's very challenging to start or grow the most important part of your business, your contact list.

So what is a lead magnet?

- Very simply, it's an irresistible bribe that gives a specific piece of value to a prospect, in exchange for their contact information, which is usually their name and email address.

What's the only goal of the lead magnet?

- The goal of the lead magnet is simple: convert traffic into leads.

The great thing about lead magnets is, they're fun to create and force you to really get inside the mind of your prospect.

Let's look at an example of a lead magnet that's working well right now. This one is for our Just Listed, Just Sold blueprint that we use to attract agents to our site.

We also have agents using it to attract For Sale by Owner "FSBO" prospects.

They give it away to FSBO's to demonstrate their expertise and to evoke the law of reciprocity.

Quick side note: don't ever worry about how you're going to drive highly targeted traffic to your ad and get them to request your lead magnet. Actually, that's the easy part.

There's a never ending stream of traffic that you can tap into for $3.00 per day, and I will go into greater detail of exactly how to set up your Facebook ad audience in the following chapters.

Ok, so once the ad is clicked by our target prospect, the prospect is sent to a landing page in order to deliver the lead magnet and get them on to our list.

Once this happens, the "ethical bribe" is consummated and a lead is generated.

Are you leveraging Facebook real estate buyer's traffic ...or just talking about it?

The four core components of a good landing page:

- Images and sales copy are relevant to the offer in the ad
- Ultra-specific
- Highly valuable to the target audience
- Easily consumed (instant access)

You can also send prospects to your blog, to a Facebook business page post and other online assets that you have in place.

Once the prospect arrives on the landing page that you see above, they click on the button to access the PDF, insert their name and email address.

After that's done, the magnet is instantly delivered to the prospect as promised and we have their email address.

Below is a snapshot of what our inbox looked like after I had my article published on Inman Select. When real estate agents clicked on a link in the article, it took them to our Lead Magnet landing page where they opted in for some highly valuable content:

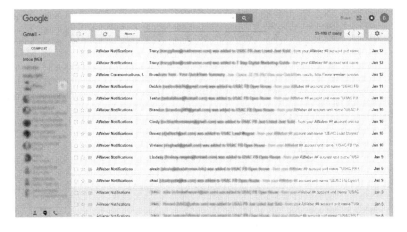

When you deliver high quality, easily consumable content that your target prospect wants, you will generate leads.

Know your target audience

Copyrighted Material

To create an effective lead magnet, you have to know what challenges your clients have, or will encounter somewhere along the home buying or selling process.

It's easy to waste precious digital ad dollars and doubt the effectiveness of lead magnets, if you don't laser focus your effort at this step.

Here's a list of the top market segments that real estate agents are currently targeting with their digital marketing dollars.

- First time home buyers
- Homeowners moving up
- Homeowners scaling back
- Luxury homebuyers
- Facebook relationship status "Divorced"

Be sure to create an Avatar for each one of these target market segments before you set up your Facebook ad campaign.

This will ensure that you positively know who you should be targeting your ad towards, and help you choose the correct options during your Facebook ad creation and set up process.

Make A Big Promise!

Now that you have identified your target market, your ability to generate leads is directly tied to the promise you make.

- You must attempt to enter a conversation that's already going on in the mind of your prospect.
- What are their concerns, fears and problems that they are sure to face?
- What is the one big promise you can make and deliver on?

As a real estate agent you have the ability to add real value to their life.

Let's review an example we created for one of our agents, who had a 62 year old couple that wanted to buy a lakefront property in Northern Michigan on Torch Lake.

Prospective buyers at the time were concerned that property values were still going down in Northern Michigan.

As a result, the lead magnet promise would go something like this:

"This two page detailed Northern Michigan Lake Front property report, will list 4 of the most sought after areas that have seen an ***increase in home value***.

The report includes links to our 3D virtual home tours, which also include audio descriptions of these lake front areas with listed pros and cons to each one"

Your ability to generate leads with a lead magnet is directly tied to the promise you make them.

You know what they don't, and they'll be happy to give you their contact information, if you're giving them tremendous stand-alone value with your lead magnet.

Creating ultra-specific lead magnets that are easily consumed

The lead magnet must be easily consumable, and since it's most likely your first interaction with the prospect, your lead magnet must be ultra-specific.

You can't offer them a 200 page book or a seven day course on home buying or selling vacation properties.

Think more along the lines of a two page PDF that has checklists and bullet points which provide instant gratification.

This lead magnet should also have your logo, head shot and contact information, along with links back to other relevant content on your blog or Facebook business page.

It should also contain linked social media images to make it ultra-simple for them, to help them share the lead magnet with their friends and family members.

One lead can become multiple leads, which is the essence of list building (generating your own leads).

Acceptable lead magnet formats

Once you have identified your target audience and made a big promise to them, it's time to deliver the magnet.

There are several effective delivery formats. Here's a few of our agents' favorites:

- Cheat sheets
- Blueprints
- Video training
- Quiz or survey with a valuable give away
- Handout
- Specific neighborhood buying guide
- Specific property type selling guide

Ultra-specific lead magnets should never be vague or general.

They have to be laser focused and offer a hyper specific solution to a known buying or selling challenge.

As Ty Webb (Chevy Chase) told his caddy, Danny, in the movie Caddy Shack, "Let me give you a little advice...Be the Ball".

Know your client. Deliver highly valuable and easily consumable lead magnets, and prospects will beat a path on to your list.

To help you do that, I've created a 7 Point Lead Magnet check list and you can download that at "http://usagentcoach.com/usac-lead-magnet-for-agents"

In chapter three, I told you about Aweber and how to set your email communications on auto pilot. If you do not follow up with your prospects, your lead generation efforts will be wasted.

Once you have generated your own leads, and are starting to build your list, you have to communicate with that list and the easiest way to do that is with Aweber or other email autoresponder software.

Chapter 7: Generate Highly Targeted Buyer Leads with Facebook Just Listed Ad Campaigns

It's time to generate your own online leads!

What does 1.44 Billion Monthly Facebook users mean? It means that half of the internet population is using Facebook daily..

You MUST leverage Facebook to explode your real estate business, and generate a steady stream of predictable leads instead of paying for them.

We created a "Facebook for Just Listed, Just Sold Properties Blueprint" for you at the end of this chapter. It's available to download as a pdf.

You can also grab it "http://usagentcoach.com/facebook-just-listed-just-sold" now if you want to print it out and follow along while reading this chapter.

As you have come to learn while reading this book, Facebook is an essential aspect of marketing for digital real estate agents.

It's imperative to approach social platforms with a strategy that's *proven to win*. It's more effective to use an organized, tested approach for achieving optimal success.

Cutting edge brokers and real estate agents that refuse to "die on the vine" with outdated marketing models, should understand these basic just listed, just sold strategies.

It's time for you or your marketing department to capitalize on the highly targeted quality Facebook traffic, by building a strong presence with your Facebook account.

> "In marketing, nothing else matters but driving traffic and converting it into a lead (list building)"

Your content (lead magnets) should be unique, intriguing, solve a problem and should be produced on a regular basis. It's a must if you want to provide quality engagement with your prospects, and attract natural internet search traffic.

For real estate listings, advertising with Facebook exposes your clients' property to thousands or millions of highly targeted users.

It has the added benefit of generating qualified leads for you and your clients' property. Usually, you can do this for less than $50.00 per listing.

We have used the word "optics" in this book several times, and have spoken about how your brand needs to be built around you.

When you incorporate this strategy into your digital listing presentation and your Facebook ad campaigns, you're telling your prospect that you're the go to digital marketing agent.

You're the expert!

When it comes to using Facebook ads for listing properties, the task may be quite daunting and confusing. Agents have challenges with setting the ads up, budgeting a perfect amount to reach your audience and adding pixels for re-targeting purposes.

Preparation before Advertising

You should have our "Facebook Just Listed, Just Sold Blueprint" in hand before you review the next section.

You can access the blueprint at "USAgentCoach.com/facebook-just-listed-just-sold"

Before you create ads, make sure that you've set up your Facebook business account, understand your ad placement options and expound on your consumer demographic targeting.

Action Steps:

- Make sure your Facebook business page is set up

- Prepare and ready an attractive call-to-action (CTA) on your Facebook page, think **lead magnet**

- Have a full comprehension of your targeted audience – know your avatar or review chapter 2

- Use technology tools like Canva, reviewed earlier in the book, to help you create and size your images for your ads

Common terms you should know when always setting up a campaign include:

- **Campaign**: refers to where you will determine the main goal of your ad and information associated with it, including URL, other accounts or addresses.

- **Ad Set**: used to establish the targeted audience that you've already budgeted for, including the time span for running your Facebook ads for listing properties.

- **Ad**: This is where you'll enter the creative aspects of your ad, such as title, headline, copy and images.

Inside your Facebook business page you will want to create your first ad in their "Power Editor" section. You will upload your high quality image, enter your headline and description of the property.

If you haven't done this yet, open your web browser and enter "facebook.com/ads/manage/powereditor" so that you can try this now.

After you have created your ad for your just listed or just sold property, make sure you are at Facebooks "Power Editor", so that you can manage and set up your ad campaign.

Here's a just sold ad example:

Once you are there at the power editor section, you will hit the "Create Campaign" button.

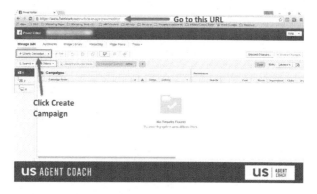

This window pops up after we have hit the "Create Campaign" button.

You want to make sure "Create New" is selected, and then enter in the just listed or just sold address of the property.

Make sure "Auction" is selected for the buying type, then "Clicks to Website" as well.

Next, hit the "Create" button and then select the "Ad Set Tab".

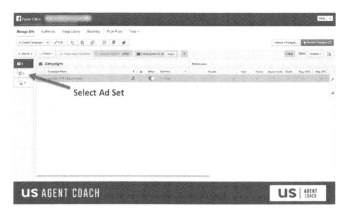

Once we are in the "Ad Set Tab", you want to select "Create Ad Set"

Make sure "Create New" is selected and for the name, you want to enter in the same name that you chose for the "Campaign Name", with "Audience Segment 1 after it".

After that, all that's left for you to do is click "Create".

Now that the ad set is created, it's time to edit it. For the daily budget, you should start off with $2 -$5 per day.

That's how you become an expert marketing tester!

For the schedule underneath the daily budget, you should set a start date for the ad to run. You should also set an end date, for one week from the start date. You should test and track your ads weekly.

Now it's time to edit your audience. This is where using Facebook gets really exciting, you can laser focus in on your target avatar prospect.

You can target the exact person that you want to see your ad.

The first thing that you want to do is enter the address of the just sold home.

Right now, I have it set to show the ad to anyone within a 15 mile radius around the home address.

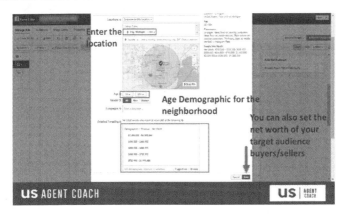

Under detailed targeting, I went to demographics, financial and then net worth and selected a 100K net worth. So unless my prospect has a net worth of at least 100k, they won't see my ad.

In the image below, under the detailed targeting section, you can see that I selected "likely to move".

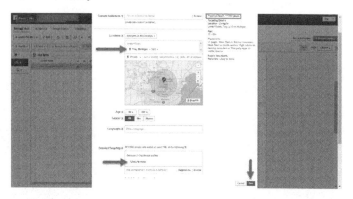

In general, this ad will target people within a 15 mile radius of the home, has a net worth of at least 100k, and had their credit pulled for a home purchase mortgage.

You can go much deeper with Facebook ad selects; the world is your oyster!

All you need to do now is hit "Save".

Be sure to print out the Facebook blueprint for Just Listed, Just Sold properties, so that you have a quick reference guide.

If you need help, you can head over to usagentcoach.com to access our digital marketing team and step by step video trainings.

If you have set up your digital assets and prepared your email (follow up) auto responders, you're ready to launch your new cutting edge digital marketing ad campaigns.

If you haven't set them up yet, get started or get some help. It's time for you to take control of your business and separate yourself from the competition.

You can begin to generate your own online leads and explode the size of your list today!

CHAPTER 8: USING FACEBOOK TO HOST A COST EFFECTIVE OPEN HOUSE

In case you didn't hear about it, Facebook had its first day user count top 1 BILLION!

In the last chapter, we went into granular detail about how to set up and target your perfect audience. The exact same technical set up, via Facebook's Power Editor, can be used to execute the Facebook Open House strategy.

For that reason, I won't bore you with the same step by step guidance in this chapter.

Agents using Facebook to promote Open House events are spending dimes instead of dollars to generate more traffic for their clients and more leads for them.

There's a link to our Facebook Open House Blueprint PDF at the end of this post for you to download.

There's no better place to find low cost, highly targeted traffic (leads) for your next Open House and for your most important asset – your list.

Remember, you need to engage buyers where they are – 99% of them are online, and almost every one of your prospective buyers will check in on Facebook today.

The debate is over; you're definitely doing your client a disservice by not promoting their open house with Facebook. Agents using digital marketing strategies and tactics spend less money and get 5-10X the desired results, when compared to Agents using outdated promotion strategies.

By using simple, cost effective digital marketing strategies, you end up attracting the exact type of buyer that's looking for your client's type of property.

You can quickly lose your client to the competition if you're not using Facebook to promote your listings.

When you show up at your listing appointment and have these ads or similar ads in your presentation, you will be showing your clients that you are not just another agent. Incorporating the data or analytics that Facebook provides into your listing presentation, will make it easy for you to win the listing, over agents with outdated marketing plans.

Think "Optics".

You also harm yourself as an agent by missing out on the opportunity to add new prospects to your list. Not every lead is going to want to go to your open house.

You can retarget each person who clicks on your ad with other ads of yours. This advanced strategy is called "retargeting" and the cost of retargeting this new "lead", is actually much cheaper on a cost per impression basis.

Have you ever wondered why after you click on a particular ad, you seem to see that same company placing ads in front of you for days or weeks afterwards?

That's the power the almighty Facebook has afforded you...the power of retargeting your leads.

Check out this piece of data from the National Association Of Realtors

Exhibit 7-1 METHOD USED TO FIND REAL ESTATE AGENT (Percentage Distribution)	All Sellers	34 and younger	35 to 49	50 to 59	60 to 68	69 to 89
Referred by (or is) a friend, neighbor or relative	38%	45%	38%	34%	38%	40%
Used agent previously to buy or sell a home	22				21	17
Visited an open house and met agent	5	5	3	5	7	5
Internet website (without a specific reference)						2
Personal contact by agent (telephone, email, etc.)						2
Referred by another real estate or broker						3
Saw contact information on For Sale/Open House sign	78% Of Clients DID NOT use their previous agent					4
Referred through employer or relocation company						*
Direct mail (newsletter, flyer, postcard, etc.)						2
Walked into or called office and agent was on duty	2	2	1	2	2	3
Newspaper, Yellow pages or home book ad	1	*	1	*	1	2
Advertising specialty (calendar, magnet, etc.)	1	*	*	1	1	*
Crowdsourcing through social media/knew the person through social media	*	*	*	*	*	*
Saw the person's social media page without a connection	*	*	*	1	*	1
Other	14	5	9	14	12	20

Do you know why there's a horrific past client return to original agent rate of just 22%?

Only two out of ten homeowners use the same agent on their next real estate transaction, which means you have an enormous opportunity to differentiate yourself and gain market share.

This should get you very excited! It's much easier for digital marketing agents to make these clients, clients for life!

When home owners were asked why they didn't use their original agent, their answer was simple: "They didn't do anything but post a sign in my yard and put it on the MLS and pray".

The three P's of outdated real estate agent marketing rears its ugly head again!

From reading the last chapter, you know that Facebook allows you to laser target ads to users that just had their credit pulled for a purchase mortgage transaction.

You know that you can set this type of ad campaign up on Facebook for $5.00 per day. That's your edge!

You also know that Facebook allows agents to target users that make a certain income, live in a specific geographic area and so much more!

You are now equipped with the knowledge to articulate your value proposition to clients, unlike 95% of the agents in your marketplace.

Take advantage of the fact that Facebook advertising is easier to use than setting up a postcard or newspaper ad campaign, costs about 80% less, and allows you to track and share your results with your client!

It's a complete waste of money to send postcards or purchase newspaper ad space, in comparison to a $50.00 Facebook Open House ad campaign.

Can you track how many neighbors actually see a postcard or newspaper
ad? **NO**

With Facebook audience/post reach can you track everything and print the results to share with your client? **YES**

How are you going to show your client that you are different from every other agent vying for the listing?

That's another great reason to master digital marketing or let our team do it for you.

You can actually show your clients the exact amount of prospective homeowners who viewed their property via social media analytics.

Showing is always better than telling...as the old saying goes, "numbers don't lie but people do".

Facebook will help you differentiate yourself from the competition, enable you to add new leads to your list with lead magnets and generate dozens of prospective buyers for your clients' home.

Proven, quantifiable results for 75-90% less than a postcard or newspaper ad campaign = Winning!

We created a blueprint that shows you the action steps necessary to take make this happen for your client in less than 30 minutes. You can access it by going to "http://usagentcoach.com/usrc-facebook-open-house-for-realtors"

Chapter 9: The Digital Agent Mindset

> A wise man adapts himself to circumstances, as water shapes itself to the vessel that contains it. --
> *Chinese Proverb*

It all starts with the willingness to surrender any pre-conceived notions about online and social media marketing.

You have to believe certain truths, that once embraced, will help you enjoy your personal and business life on a much greater level.

You can't guess what your target market wants from you, and the great news is you don't have to.

Also, you can't use general observations anymore, because the digital society only wants to "connect" with like-minded individuals.

This is good news for you, as you will only be connecting with people that are truly open to sharing their personal likes and dislikes.

Now you know how to use Facebook and you now have access to our digital marketing team if you need help!

We will be releasing our advanced Facebook ad strategies shortly, and you will get the updated version of this book.

Facebook will let you laser target your ads to groups that your target audience participates in. We allow Facebook to target all of our friends, share what groups we participate in; we allow Facebook to track everything that we do.

If you're on Facebook or have downloaded a mobile app, what's the first thing that you have to agree to?

"Accept or Reject the Permissions Code"

You, along with everyone else operating in the new world digital order, are asked to agree to share everything, or you can say "no".

You either get the program or application you want by "accepting" or choose to move up to the mountains and live off of berries and bull dung.

Web browsers, mobile applications and social media networks capture volumes of data about everything we do. It's how digital marketers laser target their ads to the exact audience they want.

Consumers are essentially self-tracking, and they're ok with it and you should be also.

It's not just on social media either...

Think about Fitbit, tracking the amount of steps you take, your heart rate, what you eat, what you drink and it goes on to tell a user how much of your sleep is in the "REM" state.

These are all signs to digital marketers; you can find out exactly what digital data your target prospect is interested in. You need to know where your prospects' attention is to achieve your goals and objectives.

It allows you to serve your digital ad, lead magnet and highly desirable content to the exact clients that you're looking to work with.

The paradigm shift has already occurred in the business of real estate and digital agents will gain more market share, faster than ever before, if they embrace reality.

Brand drivel is the death of every real estate agent, so stop wasting your time and precious ad dollars.

To get and keep the attention of your prospects, all you have to do is share your local real estate market expertise (content).

To solve problems that you know your prospects have, all you have to do is create highly valuable content, have great digital optics and prospects will beat a path on to your list!

In the next chapter, I want to share a blog post that I wrote last year. It contains a short story where I point out what FEAR actually stands for.

The last chapter is dedicated to helping you eliminate FEAR once and for all and crush it like the cockroach that it is.

Chapter 10: Crush Agent FEAR Like The Cockroach That It Is

> **fear**
> /ˈfir/
> *noun*
>
> **False Evidence Appearing Real**
>
> 1. an unpleasant emotion caused by the belief that someone or something is dangerous, likely to cause pain, or a threat.
>   "drivers are threatening to quit their jobs in fear after a cabby's murder"
>   synonyms: terror, fright, fearfulness, horror, alarm, panic, agitation, trepidation, dread, consternation, dismay, distress; More

That's exactly what fear stands for:

False

Evidence

Appearing

Real

Real estate agent fear is real; it happens to every single agent at different stages of their career.

It happens when you decide to become an agent, have to pass your state exam, present your first digital listing presentation or put up your first Facebook business page or Facebook Open House ad.

But most fear is what I call false fear. And ***those thoughts*** won't stop entering your mind unless you learn how to crush them like the cockroaches that they are.

Fearing for your life when an attacker is coming at you with a gun is real fear.

Fear of asking for your first listing contract, is a false fear, inserted into your mind from the evil one.

The first fear is real human instinct, gifted to us in order to preserve our life.

The second fear is psychological fear used by our enemy; it's his number one tool to keep you right where you're at.

He uses it to keep you from achieving what you were inspired to achieve, what your Creator inspired you to achieve. If you don't believe in God, then you can call this good energy or bad energy, or whatever you call the unseen.

The truth about fear, whether you want to believe it or not is this:

The only real fear is instinctual fear, which was infused into your being to help save your life, or escape from a very bad situation.

Instinctual fear is real and good.

This chapter is about psychological fear, and the acronym for FEAR: **F**alse **E**vidence **A**ppearing **R**eal. The psychological fear...

Psychological fear is false evidence that's entered your mind as a thought. And you can quickly crush that thought like the cockroach that it is, with a simple thought tool I'm going to share with you in a moment.

You have the full right, power and authority to do so.

Psychological fear can harm you if you focus on it. Stop inviting fear into your life now.

A good exercise to help you accomplish this is to start by writing down each fear in a notebook and put a date next to it.

You're only allowed to write these down once a week and you're only allowed to update the notebook once a week. What you'll find out in less than 30 days is that your false fears never or rarely come true.

If they come true, it's because you focused on them and manifested them into reality.

That's the power of free will; you can manifest anything into reality.

Quit inviting defeat, sickness and bad breaks into your life.

You cannot stop what thoughts come into your mind, but you can stop what thoughts you choose to ruminate on.

DO NOT COME INTO AGREEMENT WITH YOUR FEAR

Pay attention to what thoughts you are agreeing with. Be ultra-careful who you ask for advice or opinions from.

Before you ask for advice, you need to ask yourself these questions:

Is the person I'm asking advice from winning or losing in the game of life?

or...

Have they accomplished what I want to accomplish. Are they qualified, and are they going to give me encouraging and positive guidance?

If they aren't winning or have not accomplished what you want to accomplish, then save your breath. They will end up co-manifesting your false fears into reality.

You must be able to combat all of these unfounded fears. You need to decide whether or not you want to activate faith or fear.

You must commit for the rest of your life to guard your mind, and be intense about that commitment. Here's the one sentence I use to defeat the enemy's thought the second it enters my mind.

> "Do your best and God will do the rest"

You have to understand how precious and powerful your mind is, and then commit to destroying false thoughts the moment they enter.

If you're going to live in victory, you have to be disciplined in your thought life.

There's no other way to free your mind.

Quick story...

I went to an awesome therapist at an early stage of my adulthood, when my faith muscles were still weak. She would always ask me a question after I shared what I was concerned about.

"Blaise, what's the worst thing that can happen if this unfounded fear comes true?"

My answer was always something like:

I won't be able to start my business

I'll have to work for someone else's dreams

I won't be able to purchase the home in the area I want to live in

I won't attract the right love into my life

I'll have to do this…

I won't be able to do that…

This dream won't come to pass…

Nothing bad was actually happening to me. My thoughts were nothing more than confusing ***potential outcomes** t*hat I was giving power to.

That's how the enemy made me weak back then. Just like kryptonite around Superman's neck.

I want to close out this chapter with a great story that I heard while listening to a pastor I like on YouTube.

There was a big strong man named Nick, who worked for a large produce company out in their shipping yard. He was one of the company's most reliable employees, but he was also a chronic worrier.

Always fearing the worst and talking about what might happen.

One summer day, the crew was told they could leave early to attend the foreman's birthday celebration, but he didn't hear the announcement.

He was out working in one of the refrigerated box cars, where nobody could see him and somehow he was accidentally locked inside.

He didn't have a cell phone and everyone else was gone to the birthday party.

Once he realized he was locked inside, he began to panic and scream at the top of his lungs. He beat on those doors until his fists were bloody. Eventually he ran out of energy and his voice gave out.

He was very aware that he was in a refrigerated box car and ***he guessed that it was well below freezing and began to fear the worst***.

He thought, if someone doesn't save me, I'll be locked in here all night, I could freeze to death. The more he thought about it, the colder he got. Shivering uncontrollably, he found a piece of cardboard that he was able to scribble a note on, and he did, "so cold, body getting numb, these may be my last words…"

The next morning, the crew came in and found him in the box car, curled up in a ball.

Here's the amazing thing about this story…

The autopsy report revealed indeed he had frozen to death, but the refrigeration unit wasn't even on, the temperature was 51 degrees.

Nick froze to death because he was **convinced in his mind** that he was in a freezing box car. The thing he feared most came upon him.

Fear makes challenges much bigger than they are.

You need to ask yourself this question the next time false thoughts enter your mind: Are you freezing to death, even though its 51 degrees?

If you want to accomplish something great today, that's sure to crush false fears, take me up on this challenge.

I challenge you to use one of our best free blueprints that will help you set up a Just Listed Just Sold ad campaign on Facebook. I went over how to achieve success with this, in detail, throughout the book.

No excuses - If you don't have listings, then use one of your colleagues'.

It takes less than 30 minutes to do and is sure to help you strengthen your faith muscle.

You Can Find the Facebook Blueprint for Realtors at "<http://usagentcoach.com/facebook-just-listed-just-sold>"

Do your best, God will do the rest!

Made in the USA
San Bernardino, CA
30 August 2017